Study Hacks

Effective Study Hacks to Help Save Time

(Learn From the Best to Get Amazing Grades in Less Time)

Arlene Burns

Published By **Bengion Cosalas**

Arlene Burns

All Rights Reserved

Study Hacks: Effective Study Hacks to Help Save Time (Learn From the Best to Get Amazing Grades in Less Time)

ISBN 978-1-77485-667-3

No part of this guidebook shall be reproduced in any form without permission in writing from the publisher except in the case of brief quotations embodied in critical articles or reviews.

Legal & Disclaimer

The information contained in this ebook is not designed to replace or take the place of any form of medicine or professional medical advice. The information in this ebook has been provided for educational & entertainment purposes only.

The information contained in this book has been compiled from sources deemed reliable, and it is accurate to the best of the Author's knowledge; however, the Author cannot guarantee its accuracy and validity and cannot be held liable for any errors or omissions. Changes are periodically made to this book. You must consult your doctor or get professional medical advice before using any of the suggested remedies, techniques, or information in this book.

Upon using the information contained in this book, you agree to hold harmless the Author from and against any damages, costs, and expenses, including any legal fees potentially resulting from the application of any of the information provided by this guide. This disclaimer applies to any damages or injury caused by the use and application, whether directly or indirectly, of any advice or information presented, whether for breach of contract, tort, negligence, personal injury, criminal intent, or under any other cause of action.

You agree to accept all risks of using the information presented inside this book. You need to consult a professional medical practitioner in order to ensure you are both able and healthy enough to participate in this program.

Table Of Contents

Chapter 1: My Study Habits Are Not Working 1

Chapter 2: Tips For Improving Your Study Habits 13

Chapter 3: Identify Problem Parts & Areas 20

Chapter 4: Planning Ahead 42

Chapter 5: Unlocking Your Study 45

Chapter 6: Lessons At Least Twice..73

Chapter 7: Preparing Your Environment................81

Chapter 8: The Best Reading Methods 87

Chapter 9: Memory Concept 106

Chapter 10: Studying Like A Superstar 111

Chapter 11: Organizing Time 118

Chapter 12: Psychology Hacks 133

Chapter 13: Types Of Learning Styles 150

Chapter 14: Supplementation & Nootropics 165

Conclusion 184

Chapter 1: My Study Habits Are Not Working

Every student likes to have a favorite study routine. Select the one that you are most proud of:

Every important concept should be highlighted in your book

Note taking during lectures

Working all night to learn a subject

Listening to music while you're reading a book

Every 15-30 minutes, take a stretching break at the desk.

Snacks while you read

Record yourself reading a lesson while on your commute.

Chances are you've already tried at least one or more of these habits. It is possible that your study rituals are not included in this list. But the point is that studying is a highly-individualized process, since each person needs to find a certain technique that works effectively for them. All study techniques are not right for everyone.

So you tried these things, but found that you weren't really learning enough despite all your efforts. Ever wonder why?

It is possible that your preferred method may not suit you. You also might not know which learning style is most beneficial for you.

This chapter will show you why certain study habits fail, what learning styles are and how to determine your exact learning style. This will help you identify what's wrong and allow you to gently change your approach in order to adapt better study habits.

Is your study routine not working?

Stressful and challenging student life can make it difficult. You need to find a learning habit that will work for you regardless of all the challenges you may face during your student years.

Some habits work best for a small number of students at first. It can lead to a decrease in students' learning and health.

Take this as an example.

You have decided to put in an extra effort to learn a hard lesson in Physics. Your first night was a success. Even though you didn't sleep much, you still understood the material. Since then, your first night was a success; you are now able to study all night and still understand the lessons. You only eat snacks and take power naps to keep yourself energized.

Three months of nightly studying suddenly makes you feel sluggish when you go to school. You found it difficult to remember an important law in electromagnetism.

You tried to go back to your nighttime studies tonight but your brain stopped working and you can't accept the concepts.

You didn't abandon your nighttime study habits. You tried all the things you could to make nighttime study more effective.

It felt as though your brain was cheating your brain for days. Your priority list should include finding another study method.

The whole point of the example is that while it may seem like a great technique at first, you will eventually find out how it works after using it for longer periods of time.

If you're in a similar situation to me, you may need to reconsider your study methods. The best way to make smarter choices is to determine if your study routine is either too harmful or too effective. Once you've evaluated your current habits and found out what they are, you can change to a more effective method.

What are Learning Styles and How Do They Work?

Do you notice a natural preference to learn in a particular way? This is your learning method. This goes often unnoticed but is actually a dominant style that allows you to absorb more information.

These are the basic learning styles.

1. Interpersonal/Social: You enjoy being around other people. Group studies are great for your brain.

2. Intrapersonal/Solitary - You're a master of the self-study realm. You prefer to be alone when studying.

3. Kinesthetic/Tactile/Physical - You learn concepts well when you use your sense of touch. You use your body and hands to process information and explore concepts. Participating in experiments and hands-on activities can help you learn faster.

4. Spatial/Visual -- You love visuals that illustrate concepts. Learning comes from seeing things and being able to visualize them in your own head. Flashcards are great for learning.

5. Mathematical/Logical. You can understand concepts best when they have been presented in systems that employ reasoning and logic. Your greatest allies in learning are numbers and symbols.

6. Linguistic/Verbal means that you use words to help yourself learn. You tend to

retain information better by writing, reading, and taking note.

7. Auditory/Aural Learning - Your auditory/aural hearing is what you use to retain and learn information. It is how you turn information into music and sounds to help you remember and understand them. Learning is best done by listening to lectures and discussions.

Every learning style employs different parts of the brain. Researchers have observed various parts of the brain being used by people who use brain-imaging tools. This means that you can exercise your entire brain as you master different learning styles. The brain that is associated with learning styles you choose will grow as you get more comfortable.

You can exhibit multiple learning styles. It is actually quite common in people all over the world.

You may love taking down and reading notes while studying. You then read the lessons aloud to your smartphone and take notes. These notes can be used to help you grocery shop, commute, and so on. There are two types of learning that best suit you: linguistic/verbal and audio/aural.

Finding Your Learning Style

Your learning style is what you should be studying so you can make great habits. Here are the steps:

Answer dedicated questionnaires.

Find online questionnaires that will help determine your learning style. These quizzes will reveal your learning style and help you to learn more.

Expect to answer questions concerning your daily interactions with other people, your learning habits, and the way you accomplish your daily tasks.

VARK is the most accurate method you can use. VARK stands for four different learning styles.

Visual

Auditory

Reading/Writing

Kinesthetic

This test allows you to pick from several situations and will require you to decide which approach you will take to master that particular situation.

Kolb Experiential Model Best Fit Self-Assessment may also be an option. This test is built on Kolb's Experiential Learning Cycle and lists four main learning styles:

Accommodating Style-Learning through doing and feeling

Assimilation Style - Learning through watching and thinking

Divergent Style – Learning through looking and feeling

Converging style - Learning through doing and thinking

Kolb's tests require that you rank the following learning styles numerically. You should rank which style suits you best. A score of 4 signifies that it does not suit you. You will then be able to explain your reasons for choosing this style. From here, you can assess how you interact with the environment around and learn from it.

It's okay to take Kolb's and VARK tests. Remember that there is no right answer here, and that different results can be obtained for different people. You may find out that you are compatible with more than one learning style.

Start with each learning style.

You should now be able narrow your choices down to a few. Learning should be done consciously, using the learning style that is most suitable for you. Each learning style should be used for a specific time period and then you should perform a self-assessment before moving to the next. One example is to give yourself two weeks to master visual styles. Then, assess your progress and move on the kinesthetic styles.

This might seem like a tedious task, but by applying the styles in your actual studies you can really understand which ones are best for you. You can adjust your study habits accordingly to include one or more learning styles that suit you and your needs.

Sometimes, habits that have worked for you previously might not work in the long term. Understanding your learning style is key to improving your learning abilities and keeping you motivated to study for success.

Self-assessment tools will help you to discover your learning style. By trying different styles, you can find those that work well with your memory, comprehension, retention, or comprehension.

Now that you have determined your best learning method, it is time for you and your team to discover effective study methods that will allow you to gain the most from every study session. The next chapters will focus on 6 study methods and techniques. While the last chapter provides additional tips and tricks that can help you increase your study productivity.

Chapter 2: Tips For Improving Your Study Habits

Develop a Routine

Studying in the evening is a good idea. You can't do this all night. By following these steps, your body will adapt to it, and you'll be able get the best possible study strategy. Your body will be completely numb if it is forced to study over for several days or nights. You can choose one and keep it.

Get some sleep

Even if you're learning in the evening, it doesn't mean that you should sleep less. An effective study program requires an energized personality.

Get the Lighting Right

It can happen to all of us. Be careful that this doesn't become a daily occurrence. If you are a night-student, make sure to work in a well-lit place. This will help enhance your studies.

Master Time Management

It is easy not to think about time when you are studying in the evening. This makes it more crucial to set a study timetable that clearly defines when you will need breaks. It is recommended to take a break of 5-10 seconds every few minutes while you're contemplating.

Listen to Music as You Study

As we have said, the benefit of learning during the night is the increase in your innovation levels. Manny believes that their imagination is stronger in the evening. Many craftsmen continue to work into the evening because of this. Listening to music that moves or inspires you is a great way to influence your imagination.

Form a Study Group

In the dead of the night, studying is not able to provide the same social viewpoints as daytime contemplating. This is why it may be a good idea for you to set up a study group that includes other night persons to help keep you persuaded.

Finals, due dates, and exam deadlines all have one thing in common: They persuade us to skip sleep. Although it's undoubtedly not true, sometimes an all-night affair can be the right choice. If that is the case, you should be careful.

Denying your body rest is very bad. The best way to avoid being a night-owl is to "don't do that at all".

This is not a practical arrangement, and there are days when you have to work late. Even so, you should always remember that sleeping less can cause a decrease in your body's ability to get enough sleep.

Reduced slumber will make your life more difficult. There are some circumstances in which staying awake all night is not a fatality.

1. When your workload falls on the next day. It's terrible to be unable to focus on your classes or work. But, everyone has slower days. Even if your Friday deadline is Thursday, staying up later to complete a project is not nearly as harmful.

2. It is important to take time for relaxation. The best way to get sleep is to rest. If you are able to find some time to relax in the evening, staying up all night to work on a project can be acceptable. If staying up through the night means that

you won't be able to rest for 2 days, you should reconsider.

3. If you haven't done any nights studies recently, you can start working an all-nighter. Staying awake through the night can lead to a loss of sleep. If you are constantly up, it will ruin your sleeping routine forever. If you have not slept enough in the last few nights, don't go to bed until you feel refreshed.

How to Study Effectively

1. Take a walk before you go for your exam

It has been demonstrated that repetition can improve your mental abilities and memory. Your memory and intellectual abilities can be strengthened by physical activity. But, you don't have to just run on the treadmill to get better execution. Your body will love what you do. Wii can be used to get you moving, whether it's running, 20 minutes of a workout DVD, or just turning on your favorite tracks and getting your room moving like no one's watching.

2. Instead of silently reading your material, you should speak loudly

Although it may seem insane, don't be afraid to do this. You'll be amazed how much more you can remember once you've shared it so everyone can understand.

3. Reward yourself every once in awhile

There are many ways you can integrate a prize scheme into your study style. A trail of sticky bears, or your top choice, non-liquefying desserts, can be left at intervals throughout your course book or notes to motivate you to keep going.

4. Share Everything You Learned

If you want to know if something is truly understood, the best way to do so is to show it off to someone else.

Learning is about keeping information accessible so it can be used later. The best way to demonstrate something is to have it in your possession. This makes learning as if you are trying to teach it.

Chapter 3: Identify Problem Parts & Areas

I have seen students struggle with difficult sections.

These problem sections can be chapters you believe are irrelevant, but neglecting it can often lead to a loss in your overall knowledge.

Information Technology (IT), I neglected to pay attention the section on how you can successfully identify and rectify error reports when running code tests.

This was back in high school. What's more, it didn't affect my ability write code.

I was able, without any prior knowledge, to code a program for a simple task. But my inability to understand how to fix errors made it impossible for my code not work.

What good are 300 line codes if they don't provide accurate results. Very little. What I did find was that without a good understanding of the basics, or the section preceding the problem, it will be difficult to get through it. It was because I paid attention to this section that I was finally able to understand how to deal with error messages.

Simply review the contents immediately preceding the problem section and then you can attempt to learn them.

This will allow you to remember the basic concepts and help you master any problem section.

You can only overcome obstacles once you are confronted with them. It's better to deal with them during your preparation than when you're at the exam.

Allow yourself to get over these hurdles from the comfort of home or class.

So mark the problem sections and take extra time to learn them.

Master the "Easy" Stuff [-]

Y

You only get as good as your performance in the previous semester. It's reasonable to assume that your previous semester's performance was not good enough. If you fail to analyse, adapt, or transform your work before the next examination, then it will be the same result.

Each subject is different. There will be sections that are simple or hard, depending on your level.

Not just because a professor/lecturer, student, or other person tells you that you'll have trouble with a certain section, it doesn't necessarily mean it won't apply to you. No matter what others have experienced, the determining factor is your personal experience.

I'm not saying to ignore other people's experiences. But, it is important that you use the information to make informed decisions about how much of your time and effort you'll devote to a particular situation.

I have seen too many students rely on others' experience only to fail their tests.

You are on an individual journey.

Learn by trial and error what is simple and what is challenging during the learning stage. However, once you've practiced answering questions and learned the answers, I urge you to make a note.

This is important because it will help you to understand the sections you find the easiest when you get to the revision stage.

Why?

It's just to ensure that the sections you are studying yield results. I don't spot-learn, but it helps you to master a section and be able answer questions when they do appear in an examination.

Another reason I tend to master easy stuff is because it tends to the fundamental or foundational portions of a subject.

The result is that mastering these sections puts you in a favorable position to learn, comprehend, and master the detailed and oriented concepts that will follow.

You build a house from the bottom.

A strong foundation will ensure that your house can withstand weather conditions like rain, wind, earth shifting, and so forth. To the same extent, once you understand the foundation of any subject, all other subjects can be learned thoroughly.

When you know things, you can recall them on demand. It is possible to recall information at will, which can make it easy for you to surprise others during examinations.

This brings us back to the crucial question of how do you learn difficult subjects. The next section will provide a critical technique for students to use that we'll discuss.

-] The Feynman Technique

I

This technique is great and you will love it.

It allows you to not only master the easy stuff but also makes difficult information simple.

Let's not get too excited and let's just focus on the technique. Many dynamic concepts are often the result of smaller ones. They are the foundation of the dynamic concept. These concepts, however, can be broken down into smaller pieces that provide more information and foundational information.

If you could understand each piece in its individual form, you'd have no problem understanding the puzzle when it is all put together.

The Feynman Technique is essentially that a student must reduce complex concepts to the simplest, simplest, and most basic explanation. Asking certain questions is one way to accomplish this:

Why?

How?

When?

What is the reason?

Let's take a closer look at this example.

Sugary biscuits are high. Okay, but why are biscuits sugary? What is the secret to making biscuits? What makes biscuits so sweet?

When you ask questions it forces you into searching for answers. If you search for answers it will bring up additional questions and related concepts. As a result, the idea that biscuits contain high amounts of sugar grows.

Once you've answered the above questions, you can then move on to answering related questions.

Is it possible that biscuits can be unhealthy? Why are biscuits unhealthy?

How would you feel if you saw that? Simply stating that biscuits were unhealthy led to the questioning about why biscuits contain high levels of sugar. This led the discovery of artificial ingredients, which in turn led to the economic dissections of biscuit production.

A topic as complex as biscuit manufacturing can be broken down to its simplest form. For example, the ingredients that go into making biscuits. This example shows that one concept can be directly applicable to another. You can also learn complex information by asking questions.

Feynman has many aspects.

It promotes simplicity, by using keywords to define concepts, drawing similarities through questions and interconnecting idea.

Simple concepts can be the starting point for complex topics.

If you can effectively break down a topic fraction by fraction, you will grasp the whole topic with no difficulty.

This method is simple: grab some paper, take out your Google and Google books, pull out a page, and start asking WHY.

Complete five cycles of WHY. Then, answer the remaining questions. After the fifth cycle, you should either have the entire topic in its simplest form or identified all the relevant concepts.

Tip - Use the Feynman Method to teach a concept instead of to yourself. Imagine how you would explain it to someone else in a simple and understandable way.

-] Note Making Styles [-

Those who think they can study an 800-page textbook without making notes are either lazy, fooling theirself or very naive. It has been shown that an average reader absorbs 10% of what they read first time.

Notes allow you to make a book less than 800 pages. This makes it more manageable and easier to study during exam season.

Notes serve a dual purpose.

To save important information and to simplify complex ideas.

For exam preparation.

Many books have to deal with complex language, jargons and fluff. It is not easy to do. Ideas and thoughts are difficult to put down on paper. Making notes is essential to benefit over the long term.

It forms part of active learn. It is not just about reading and breaking down complex text into simpler forms. You also transfer these simplified forms onto paper. This improves your likelihood of this information being embedded within your long-term memory.

Notes come many forms.

Linear notations are ideas usually represented in point forms. They are often not in detail but follow a certain order of appearance. As you read and study, you will simplify ideas into short sentences.

Simple. Clean. Effective.

This method is what I use to make notes on theoretical subjects. It saves me lots of time, makes it easier to repeat the same thing over and is simple to scan for quick reference.

One other form of note making is to highlight and extract text from quoted texts. These can be used as needed. These are things that you have likely used during your school years, so I won't waste any time.

Simple illustrations are another way to take notes that is practical and useful. Many people use 'spider Diagrams' and "root Diagrams" to show how interconnected ideas are broken down. These can be extremely useful if you're trying to visualize how everything fits together.

You can see how this note-making technique is used in this image. Nicole Walker.

These days, infographics as well as charts seem to be quite popular. This type of content is popular on many websites. Informationgraphics are a popular content type that is often shared on websites.

You can use it if it's working! Is that right?

And it works.

Charts and infographics combine relevant text with relevant images showing important messages. They even combine both linear and spider notes to create one infographic.

If you're able to design your own infographics/charts/graphics, do it! You'll improve your understanding and be better prepared for your examinations.

My concern is that anyone who has enough interest in creating an infographic/chart is committed to great results.

Below are links to some sites that allow you to create infographics using just a few buttons. I've used them quite a few times, and they've been great.

Additionally, there are many graphic options.

They are available for you to explore and use. You can also save the infographics to your computer and print them.

www.canva.com/create/infographics

www.piktochart.com

www.venngage.com

www.infogr.am

-] Time Allocation and Safety Measures for Exam Preparations [-

A

You can't cram your notes or information in the day or night before an examination. This is a recipe to failure. This technique is amazing for someone who is willing and able to put their whole exam preparation on the line.

It's something that happens to many students. This seems like a sensible thing to do. All the information will be fresh in one's head.

Wrong! But it's wrong! If you are willing to spend 3 weeks, or at least 2 weeks, studying for the exam, then you have ample time to go through your textbook, take notes, and to memorize important principles.

You don't always have to study.

In fact, if a consistent study program was followed over the previous months or even weeks, there is a good chance that you won't have any need to scramble for notes the night before. Because you've already absorbed substantial amounts of information while reading, studying, taking notes, and revising.

Even if you're preparing for an exam, the pomodoro strategy should be used. To prevent burning out, do 25-minute cycles followed by a break.

Be prepared for a difficult exam. It's important that you study well. Get enough sleep before your exam, take a good meal to fuel you body, and drink plenty water.

As it provides me with energy and mental alertness, I often take a small sachet BIOPLUS just before each test.

During the week, if you feel dizzy, lightheaded, or like your brain is leaking out of your head, stop!

Go for a stroll, do some exercise or go to bed. These are the signs that you could be entering a state of mental and possibly even physical exhaustion.

Set Goals

It is important to set goals as a learner. What are you looking to get out of this subject study?

Do you:

Are you looking for a comprehensive understanding?

Do you want the foundations?

Want to master all aspects of the subject?

Based on your choices, you can adjust your study schedule to help you reach your goals.

You can break up your book into small groups. For instance, you might read two chapters each day until your book is complete. It is a substantial amount information spread over a longer period of time that allows you digest, understand, apply and adapt what you learn.

Let's move on to goals for a second. Why is this important? When I started studying law, it was hard for me to see the end of the road. I was unaware that the assignments, exams and tests are only temporary.

Even though it might seem like a burden, or an unwelcome chore at times; studying can actually be a blessing. If you put enough effort into learning and set goals to achieve amazing results, you will ensure your success and happiness in the future.

It is only a three- to four-year journey. A career that is rewarding and remarkable can emerge after the period of study.

This is what you need to keep in mind as you set academic goals.

There is a goal. It's your career.

Your career can make you the person you always wanted to be. You decide how much work, and how much suffering, you are able do right now to help build an amazing career.

The Art Of Periodical Review

Throughout my high school years, the challenge I faced was to transfer what I had learned from short term memory and long term memories.

Naivety led me to believe that cramming would be an effective way to recall formulas and details for an examination. I was wrong.

This technique promotes recalling information years after the fact. It's simple and effective. This technique is not dependent on any magical brain techniques or voodoo.

Repeating a sentence over and over can help you remember it. It might not be perfect but it will help you remember important information. The problem lies in not knowing how much you remember from source material.

Reviewing comes in handy here.

You can make sure you read the sections you don't remember often so you can review them again.

Daniel Wong, a very successful guy, taught me how to use this technique. I found it through his review system.

Review intervals that are optimal

1 day after learning the new info

Three days after the original review

7 days from the second review

21 days after third review

30 days after the fourth evaluation

45 days after the fifth inspection

60 days after the sixth evaluation

I enjoy using this system because it has questions and answers that closely match what is being studied. You won't be offended if I say that I don't recommend studying only past year papers. However, if enough questions were answered from each section using the fundamental principles taught, it would surprise how easy it is to learn more detailed sections.

Maximum review encourages comprehension and recollection.

Chapter 4: Planning ahead

Sometimes bad memory is just because of your limiting beliefs. Renew Yourself with positive beliefs.

Even though you might not have known this, studying, like any other task that anyone may wish to undertake, requires a plan. Benjamin Franklin's famous saying, "Failing planning is the best way to fail" is very relevant. Avoid making a habit out of not planning before you dive in to anything.

Plan your future. Be clear on what you want to do in the near and long-term. Your short-term goal might involve understanding the notes you read in the next hour. At the end of the term, your long-term goal could be passing the exam. It would be helpful to write down your goal if you are clear about it. It is important to make a habit in writing down all the important information. It is important to make sure that your goals are SMART. If they are not, you might not be capable of achieving what you desire.

It is a smart idea for you to create a schedule. It allows you to see how much time it takes to accomplish your tasks. While you can plan your time and allocate the right amount of time for what should be done, it is important not to overextend yourself. You should limit your study time to no more than an hour. It is possible to think you are still studying the same subject after 2 hours. However, in most cases, you will not understand what you are learning.

Your weaknesses, limitations, strengths and goals must all be considered in your plan of actions. By focusing on your strengths, you will be able to spend less time and use that time to improve areas that are less important. Spending hours learning something you don't understand in thirty minutes would not serve any purpose.

Chapter 5: Unlocking Your Study

Your approach to studying is crucial for any subject to be understood.

However, many students make a mistake of using the identical study techniques for every subject.

Analyse and Pre-planning

The first step is to plan and analyze your study.

You should analyze your subjects and choose the right topics to focus your studies.

Knowing what to learn and how much to learn will help you design your study plans. This will also help you choose smart study techniques.

For instance,

When you are studying for a test there is no need to study everything in your textbook.

You will only need to know what the syllabus requires.

It is important not to spend too much time on miscellaneous information contained in the textbook.

If your goal to only study for the exam

Find out which type of questions you'll be asked. As per the examination point, you will need to divide your topics based on their priority or weight.

You can get an idea by looking at the question papers from previous years. Once you've identified your end goal, it is easier to plan. You can then plan how much time and energy you'll invest in this subject.

Take along your study material and make sure you learn from the best! Get the support of your teachers, friends, and family when you are struggling.

Remember that each subject is different.

Each subject requires a different learning strategy to understand it better.

Smart Techniques cannot be used for both science and history. These subjects are very different so the approaches and study techniques will differ.

It is possible. Depending on the topic, you might need more than one smart method for a given subject.

Key Points

I'm still reading math! Math is not to just be read. It must be practiced!

It is not possible to use the study strategy you used for maths to study history. The Strategy that is used to study science cannot be used.

You will be able to use the smart study techniques in this book if you take the time.

Technique #1

#1 - Self Quizzing

This is an efficient study technique that can help to recall and retain the concepts.

It helps you to save your time.

This technique can be used to help you learn about a particular topic.

After that, take a few seconds to look at the text but ask some thought-provoking question.

Write down the questions you have asked.

This allows you concentrate on the essential idea of the topic.

Try to break down a chapter of a topic or topic you have chosen. It is possible to divide it into paragraphs and pages.

Next, do what it says: Read it once or twice.

Consider the type of questions you would ask for a test or quiz, but don't look at the text. This includes -

'What is chapter/paragraph's main context?

"What are the main points?

"What is new for you?"

"What did I already know?"

Write down the answers.

Verify your answer at the conclusion.

It will make you feel more confident to write your answers. Your answers can be verified to determine the strength or weakness of the topic.

This study technique is extremely useful when there are large portions to cover. Studying in small groups can help you reduce stress.

Quizzing is an effective way to prevent forgetfulness. Forgetting is part of our human nature. Do not underestimate yourself by failing to test it. By asking questions, you can find your strengths and weaknesses within the topic.

It also provides an overview of your current knowledge and the amount you need for further study.

These unfilled templates may be downloaded here

Technique #2

Isn't that frustrating when you forget the things you have learned?

When you get all ready for an exam, and then you hit the revision, it is obvious that you have forgotten most or all of your study.

You will end up looking at it again.

Many students fail to remember the information they learned in class, even though they study well. They get confused and question everything.

Hence, why don't you keep them in mind?

Our memories can be complicated. Although we may recall some trivial facts from many years ago, our memories can quickly forget the details that we just read minutes ago.

It is because of the way our memories are categorized into short term or long term memories. Each time a new piece information is received it is saved to short term memory.

Short term memories lose their value over time. They can only be recalled once in a while.

If short term memories are recalled, they become a lasting memory. These memories are then stored for a longer time.

Each time we receive information via our senses (eyes/ears), they are lost.

These memories, however, can be retained in short term memory. These memories eventually fade.

If the same memory is frequently retrieved. If it is recalled multiple times.

This memory can be transferred to long term memory. Information is stored for longer periods.

Your brain is your computer. The file you place in a computer is processed and saved. But each computer has its own way of working.

If that data isn't used, it gradually erases the fragments. If the data is important, it recognizes them and retains them.

This is similar how our memories work.

The information should be remembered frequently and repeatedly to preserve it.

Here, we use the Spaced Repetition Technology. This is the most powerful technique to increase your brain's recall. This technique can help you transform short term memories into long term memories.

Technique #2

Spaced repetition

Spaced repetition is about creating time intervals between study session. In essence, it is a way to study multiple times but still allow time for rest between sessions.

We do this by scheduling revisions.

This basically means that once you've finished with a topic, you can plan your revisions. Next, plan your time for revisions.

One example is that you may be assigned to a topic for today. After two days, your 1st revision can be scheduled.

The second revision should be done within 4 days of the original revision.

3rd revision after 8 days and so on.

This will allow you to strengthen your memory, and increase your recall.

Aristotle says, "Repeatingly recalling one thing improves memory"

You should spread your time intervals. You can't allow enough time between revisions. This is just another boring learning experience. You need to make space in your study so that you avoid repetitive and mindless repetition.

This is the most effective memory technique. This allows you to retain the concepts in your brain for longer. This will help you to remember them well.

How to use this technique

Step 1 – Study a topic.

Step 2: Schedule your revise.

Step 3: Take a moment to reflect on each revision.

Step 4 - Review topics you are not familiar with.

Use your phone calendar to remind of your revision plans. Make sure to score yourself and evaluate your quiz responses.

You can also use the quiz questions from the earlier technique.

These unfilled templates may be downloaded here

Technique #3

Random Problem Method

Mixing things up

This technique lets you explore more than one topic at once.

You might, for example, study multiple types of maths and formulas while you are studying physics. This will allow you to switch between problems that require different solutions.

Doing a quiz on different problem types helps your brain differentiate between concepts better. You can improve your memory association.

Mixing things up will force you to constantly test your ability to identify the problem type.

Take a batsman for cricket who swings at 20 fastballs, followed by 20 slower and 20 spinballs. This type will perform better than players who use a variety of pitches.

The player who takes part in different types of training, such as swinging at different pitches, improves his ability for deciphering and responding to each ball, becoming a better batter.

The Random Problem Method's result will help you succeed in future tests.

While this may sound counterproductive or unproductive, it can actually cause confusion and misinterpretation of concepts. However, the opposite is true.

To improve your learning abilities, you should be encouraged to study more than just one subject.

It is important to know which method you should use for similar problems when taking exams.

Mixing problems will help you determine how to tackle a problem and which strategies to employ.

For example, in math. The key skill to solving a problem is to use the correct method. This is why many students have poor math skills. Because they become confused about similar problems, and then try to use a strategy for the problem that isn't meant for them.

This technique allows you to recognize it. Interleaving will help you improve that skill.

Instead of solving 10 multiplications problems, instead solve 10 divisions and 10 additions. Mixing them helps you recognize the similarities and the differences between problem types.

It helps you understand older concepts and helps you choose the right strategy for solving problems.

How to use

You can choose a topic like a math issue. Identify the number of different problems or formulas you have.

Next, you must identify what makes them distinct and how.

These steps are very similar

Combine the problems and formulas to solve them.

Recommendations?

Technique #4

SQ3R strategy

These days, there are many options for study materials.

Some videos, some audios, and the majority of study materials are in written form.

Sometimes, you may have pages of information. It's difficult to get through all of this information. If you don't understand how to optimize what is being read, understanding the material and staying on track becomes more difficult.

This method will simplify your reading and make it easier to remember, understand, or study written information quickly.

SQ3R means -

Survey,

Question,

Read,

Recite it,

Review.

Step #S: Survey

The first step is this:

You should take some time to study the topic.

Attention should be paid to the topic's structure. This includes the layout, main point, heading, subtitle, or other subtopics.

In general, try to understand what is going on in the topic's main context.

It takes usually only a few moments.

Step #Q Questions

Once you're done scanning.

Ask yourself questions.

Consider yourself an examiner who's trying to set up a question board. For example, you might convert headings or subheadings into questionable questions.

Next, you will ask yourself questions that are more general, such as

What's this chapter all about?

How can this information be of help to me?

What is this chapter trying teach you?

What did my brain already know?

Draw a vertical line along the paper. Now write your questions and answer them on either the left or right.

Step #R1 -- Read

After answering all questions, you can move on to the next step. Next, begin to read actively.

Try to pay attention to chapter headings and explanations as you read. This step is to make sure you are reading the entire topic and not just skimming.

You can always add more questions as you go. While you're reading, make sure to answer all previous questions.

Take the time to understand more complex topics.

Passive and active reading are two different things. In passive reading, you don't read much but engage in the topic deeply. Active reading is when you pay attention to the topic, and engage deeply with it.

Step #R2- Retrieve

This is the part where you try to recall what information you've learned using your own words. You will try to sum up the concept.

This can either be done orally or by writing. It is up to you. A simple explanation to someone is one of best ways to remember and ensure you understand the topic.

As a teacher, you are trying to teach the child.

Albert Einstein said, "If you can't simplify it, you don't know it well enough."

Albert Einstein used to say that his complex theory of relativity was explained by the phrase, "When one man sits for an entire hour with a beautiful girl, it feels like a minute." Let him, however, sit on a hot burner for a while. It will take more than an hour. That's relativity."

Step #R3 -- Review

This is your final step. After you've reached the end,

Go back through all sections.

Review your answers, and then verify them.

As you review the material, repeat to yourself what was read.

Surveys are a great way to prepare for your studies and therefore priming the brain.

This Template is not yet filled out can be downloaded here

Technique #5

However, you have learned the skills necessary to understand the topic and not rote-learn it. There are also certain facts that will need to be recalled.

Information such as the names and colors of the planets, the spectrums of colors, mathematical operations ordered, trigonometric proportions. Sometimes they are easy to remember and sometimes not.

It becomes more difficult to remember complicated facts like the names of bones found in a human skull.

Mnemonic devices make it possible to remember any fact.

Mnemonic devices

So, what exactly are Mnemonic Equipments?

Mnemonic Devices, also known as Memory Cues, are Memory cues that make it easy to remember facts and large amounts.

They can be combined to make a song or a syllable.

They usually consist of an acronym, or a phrase, as well as a sentence.

Mnemonics make it easier to recall facts, and are especially useful when order is critical.

As a mental file cabinet, they can be described as a place to store your information. This is where you keep your information. You can access it whenever you need.

Let's now look at some of the examples for how to use a Mnemonic.

To learn the names of all planets in an orderly manner:

Mercury, Venus Venus Earth Mars Jupiter Saturn Saturn Uranus Neptune Pluto

Just for this purpose, I just need to remember.

My Very Educated Mother cooked us nine delicious pizzas

Do you recognize the first letters of these words?

M - Mercury

V - Venus

E - Earth

M – Mars

J - Jupiter

S – Saturn

U - Uranus

N - Neptune

P = Pluto

You don't have to include pluto.

My Very Educated Mother Helped Us Nacho's

These are complex facts, like naming the bones inside a human head.

A skull is composed of six bones.

Ethmoid.

To be able to recall them from front to back.

Old People from Taxes Eat Spiders

Mnemonics devices are a great way to improve your learning efficiency. They aid in remembering things quicker, better, longer and easier.

You can see more examples here

You can remember the Electromagnetic Spectrum by using this acronym/sentence.

Venus invaded By Raging Martians With X-ray Guns

The order in accordance with which the frequency of the electromagnetic spectrum increases is:

Radio,

Microwave,

Infrared,

Visible,

Ultraviolet,

X-rays

Gamma rays.

Learn Why You Should Study

You can improve your knowledge and skills by adopting a positive attitude. You won't be able to grow watermelon seeds if you don't plant cucumber seeds. Same goes for a negative attitude. If you desire to succeed, don't be afraid of failure.

When you are determined to learn something, it is important that you approach the subject with a positive attitude.

If you think this way, it'll be boring and hard for you.

Do not assume others will agree with you.

If they say that this subject can be difficult, it is probably true. You shouldn't assume it will be easy. Try it. Try it out before you make a decision. You may find it easier than what others find difficult.

Never Limit Yourself:

Students underestimate their potential quite often. Students who have great potential and are capable, not only by others, but also by their own beliefs, can limit their potential.

"I can't do this."

"This is too much. "

"I am not that intelligent. "

Many people are not hindered by their inabilities. Instead, their beliefs can stop them from reaching their goals.

They have a predetermined belief that they won't succeed beyond this point.

They are not content with aiming higher or trying to improve.

Aim higher than yesterday to stay motivated. Do less than you did yesterday. You don't necessarily have to do all of it at once. No matter what you do, just do it 1% better today than yesterday. You can do great things if you believe in yourself and work hard to achieve them.

It is a belief that you have the ability to learn any subject that interests you.

Always aim to the Moon.

Chapter 6: Lessons at Least Twice

Learn every lesson at least two times if you really want to understand the information in a class. To learn more about a topic in a lecture, you should start reading about it Monday. Be prepared for class by knowing as much as possible about the topic you're learning. It will not waste of your time.

The advantage of knowing the information before you start lectures is that you can consolidate it, use it in your own life, and then relate it to what else you have learned. I guarantee that you'll lose some of the information you learn in every lecture. You will miss out on important information. Even more so if you are sitting next to the person who makes fun of every powerpoint slide. You can also sit next to two people who talk about their social lives.

This policy of learning serves as a great training ground for life. Your own teacher will teach you most of what you learn when you're not in school. The more you learn to teach yourself, the simpler your life will become. I've spoken to hundreds of people who have graduated high school about this. All agreed that learning how to learn is the most important lesson you can take away from school. This is what's known as "auto didactic" (auto-diedactic) learning. An autodidact is someone who self-teaches. Autodidacts have the highest intelligence and success rates in the world. You can become one.

Chapter Highlights

* Be able to learn information on the internet before you have to take it in class.

* Become an autodidact.

You can set aside time

This topic was covered at the end the "Get Organized Section", but I felt it was so important, that I want you to repeat it. Set aside a time for each assignment. Do not schedule it for more than you can afford. Do the work at the time scheduled. Achieving good grades means that you complete all assigned work, such as reading, studying, or completing an assignment, on time.

Find the value of what you do

(So that you feel motivated to do the job)

America considers the value of a product based on its price. Did you know that an expensive product can be more valuable than one that is less expensive, even though they may be identical? I've heard people say, "Wow that's a pricey bottle of wine. It must be good!" This logic often applies to education. Public school is an example. It's free and often taken as a given. Because of its low cost, it has little value. This isn't the place for discussion about public school. I have a lot to talk about, but I believe that anyone can learn a lot by working hard in a public school. Although it takes more effort to learn the same information from a top private school, this is not the point. The point is that you get more out of the effort you put in than you do.

If you don't believe in what you're learning, you will not be motivated to continue studying it. You might think that the desire for a college education is enough to justify paying for it. But, it might not. There are better motivators. You will succeed in class if there is a reason that you feel passionate about the subject.

You should take time to evaluate the benefits you will receive from any class before signing up. Are you passionate about the subject? Do you require the information to take a later class? Can what you're studying make a positive difference in your daily life? If you don't have the time or resources to take the classes required for your degree, what are your options? Are there people you know who are interested in the same subject as you? Are there any other rewards for taking the class? You can take a moment and think about the benefits. You'd be surprised at how many you can find if they aren't already.

Choose whether you should be studying alone or with a group

I study almost exclusively alone, as I find it more productive. The exceptions are only two. If I don't have the knowledge I need, but still want to master it, I seek out a group with similar interests and teach them my knowledge. If my motivation is low or I have difficulty understanding the material, I can also study in a class. If I'm taking history, philosophy, or another similar class, I will often study with others to learn from different points of views.

Everyone learns differently, so it is worth taking some time to reflect on whether you would prefer to study in a group or solo. This applies to every subject and each class. What will make the most of your time and give you the best chance to grasp the information you need in the fastest amount of time? Whatever it is: Do that.

Decide Your Best Note-Taking Strategy

The following four strategies are my favorites for taking notes.

1) Use an old-fashioned pen and notepad. This will make the method more effective. It's best to create a shorthand. Use an example: a + or the & for and to shorten long words. You should leave out the meat

of what your recording. If you feel the necessity, you can revise your notes later.

2) Write down notes on the computer. This is a great method to quickly type and take complete notes, even without ever looking away at the whiteboard or teacher.

3) Record the lecture to take notes and then record it again. This method allows you to pause or rewind lectures and allow you to listen twice. The downside is that you will spend a lot more time making notes. This may not be the most efficient use of your time. Dependent on the lecture, it can be disadvantageous to listen twice. You might believe that you can just "always get the information via the lecture recording," but this could lead to you not taking the time to learn the information you really need.

4) You don't need to take notes during class. Instead, you can compile and study the information outside of class. This method has the advantage of allowing you to memorize all information, which will make it easier for you to remember everything. It is not easy to memorize all the information and it can take a lot of time.

Your class will likely determine the best note taking strategy. Consider each class separately and test different strategies. You may find the best one.

Chapter 7: Preparing Your Environment

Your time is important and you must make the most of it. The environment where this happens will have a major impact on how productive you are. This is why it is so important to choose the best place for you to feel most comfortable and productive. It is okay to experiment with different settings, depending on your needs. Your bedroom might not be the best place for you if your study is done from home. The study, the dining and garage are all options.

If you study in a residential environment, you might feel that your room is too noisy or claustrophobic. The library, a class, a quiet coffee shop are all options. You may also want to consider reading and taking notes in the park, depending on the weather.

Be comfortable but not too comfortable. It is important to have a well-functioning work station, desk, and chair. A comfortable armchair or sofa, or even worse, a bed with books or laptop on it, will not be conducive for productive study sessions. It is important that you have a cool and comfortable work environment. Being too cold will make you feel uneasy and make it hard to concentrate. If you're too warm you can become tired and lethargic as well as sleepy, which will make it harder to concentrate. If you cannot control the temperature in your environment, or if you prefer reading in a library instead, then dress accordingly and find a spot that you feel most at ease while you study.

Your environment is predetermined before you even start classes or lectures. If you are given the choice of where you will sit, make sure to get as close as possible.

This will give you a clearer view, better hearing, and a better overall experience. There will be fewer other students within your sight line to distract you.

You don't need to worry about what stigma exists among students for sitting at front of class. Keep your feet on the ground and try to absorb as much information as possible. You shouldn't be afraid of asking questions. The lecturer will notice that you are interested in the subject matter and will be more open to answering your questions.

Distractions

Effective study requires distraction. To avoid distraction, eliminate everything that can distract you.

Many people find they need to work in quiet areas to concentrate. Others report being easily distracted in quiet environments as they cannot hear any sudden sounds. But, in noisy environments, they are able screen out continuous noise and can ignore distracting sounds. The same principle applies when it comes to movement. While some may find moving around distracting, others will not.

Are you able to focus on music or is it distracting? This is another example of how "different strokes can be applied to different people." You'll have to find out the truth for yourself. There are many studies out there that have found different results. The consensus is that light background music works well for most people and sometimes even helps with memory retention. However, it is not recommended that you listen to heavy, loud music while studying.

Be sure to get rid of all distractions and interruptions before you start studying. Be sure to clear your desk of books and gadgets. It is not a good idea to have the television on while you work. It is best to turn off your mobile phone and leave it behind. While you are working on your computer, close Twitter, Facebook, Skype and other email accounts. This will distract you from the task at hand and make it difficult to focus. You have to forget about all other distractions during your study time. Focus on your study materials 100%.

To avoid frustrating interruptions that can be persistent, make sure your friends and family know where and when you're studying. Interruptions distract from your study and cost precious time.

If you are a clock-watcher, it is best to get rid of any display of time. You can set the alarm on your smartphone to tell you when you should take a break or when to finish your studies. Switch on the light, close the curtains, and you might find yourself gazing out at the windows more often than you do the work.

Chapter 8: The Best Reading Methods

Students need effective study strategies, as well as correct reading strategies. Some students think reading is simply about scanning through notes to the end. This is the greatest mistake a student could make.

Studying academic books requires focus and total attention. To grasp concepts, you have to dig deep. Similar to eating a steak of beef, it is important that you chew the meat thoroughly before you are able to appreciate the flavor. Reading novels is far easier than studying academic materials. Reading novels is much easier than reading academic materials. The plots are what interests readers.

What are the best techniques for reading? Experts recommend the SQ3R. The acronym stands out for Survey, Questions,

Read, Recite and Recall. Let's look at it one-by-one.

Survey

Your purpose in this stage is to familiarize yourself with the content of each chapter or book that you are required to read. Check out the outline, goals, and opening questions.

Next, take a look at the figures.

Final, read the summary for each chapter.

Question

Once you've got a general idea of what the chapter is about it's time for you to read the first section. Be careful not to skip the rest of the chapter. Try to formulate a query based upon the section's header. The title and content of the section will dictate the question you form. This process will help you remember the content much better.

Read

Now that you have formulated a question, it is possible to continue reading the entire chapter. As you continue reading you will realize that you aren't only reading, but also answering the questions. It is crucial that you make notes while reading. Many students like to highlight their books while reading. They think that it helps them remember what they are reading. But, the truth is that highlighting might not be very helpful in retrieving information or memorization. Why? Because it doesn't involve any cognitive process. Highlighting words requires no mental effort. Highlighting could be helpful in identifying key points, information and sections of the chapter. However, it will not aid in memorization.

Recite

Although it sounds silly and unnecessary, reciting the material aloud is a powerful method of understanding it better. It'll be easier to see if you fully grasp the subject matter if you can recite it. Don't assume that you already understand the material. Many students experience this when they think they are familiar with the material but then find out they have no idea how to explain it. Reciting can be a huge help.

Recall/Review

Now that you have completed the chapter, it is time to go back and review. Remember all of the chapters that you've just finished reading. You can do this best by answering any sample quizzes provided at the end. If sample quizzes are not provided in the book, it is worth looking for the author's site. They often have additional material that relates to their published works. For more learning resources, see http://psychlens.com.

You will be able identify any areas that were missed. It will be easier for you to see which sections of the material need more reading. It is possible to save time and stay organized.

How to become a Memory master

Students always find it difficult to have a photographic memory, or to retain more information from what they read. This type of memory can be difficult to achieve. There are techniques that students can employ. These techniques can be used by professionals as well to make their work more productive and efficient.

The most effective and leading tip that anyone can use to remember things is the mnemonic. This technique does not seem to be new. This technique was used by Roman as well as Greek orators to give public speeches.

Here are the top mnemonics:

1. Linking

You must make a list to be able to recall a set of information. Here are some examples:

"Mercury served as the messenger god. He carried lots and lots of love notes to Venus. Venus, a beautiful goddess, sprang form the Earth's waters. She was married to Mars her brother. That didn't please her dad Jupiter or Saturn, and Uranus complained the sea god, Neptune." Saundra K. Ciccarelli

This is just a small example. There are many ways you could do this. It is important to gather all relevant information in one string and form a story.

2. Method using the "peg-word" method

This trick requires that you memorize the series or numbers of peg words. These words will then be used later to remember random information. Here are some examples of common words that can be used as peg words.

One is a muffin

Two is the definition of a shoe

Three is a Tree

Four is a door

Five is a hive

Six is bricks

Seven is heaven

Eight is a key

Nine is a Line

Ten is the number of a hen

Imagine you're at the grocery store and you don't want one item to go missing. Here's a simple example of how to use this method.

"If the items that are to be remembered include cheese, milk. eggs, bread, salt, and sugar, the series might consist of a bread roll with a wedge of cheese, a shoe with milk pouring through it, a shoe made from milk, a loaf of bread with eggs hanging from it and a hive containing little bags of sugar. The images are very bizarre and can help cement your memory. All the person needs to do when retrieving the list is to recite: "One, a bun, cheese." Two is a shoe...

3. Loci

Back then, making lengthy speeches without holding any kind of device was difficult. But the good news is that ancient peoples, especially the Romans & Greeks, are very good at memorizing speeches.

Loci, or the Roman Room Method, is one of the most popular methods. To use this method, you will need to create a mental picture of the room or area that is most familiar to you. You will need to place each information you are trying to remember in specific places within the room.

"For instance, if you were to focus on military spending, an image might show a soldier standing in front the house's doorway, tossing money into the street. Each point has its place. A person could simply take a "mental tour" around the house to get the memories back.

4. Verbal/rhythmic organization

This technique helps to recall information by using words. Verbal Mnemonics are different from visual mnemonics. Instead of actual systems, they are specific techniques. These techniques include rhymes, acrostics, acronyms, and rhymes that group together information in a meaningful way.

Acronyms are words that contain the first letter of the word you want to remember. The first letters must form meaningful words or words. This is important so that you can remember the information.

ROY, G-BIV is a common acronym that's used to remember colors. This stands as the seven primary colors, which are Red, Orange and Yellow, Greens, Blues, Indigos, and Greens.

The Simple Act That Increases Long-Term Memory

You should keep as much information about yourself as you possibly can, regardless of whether you are a student. Daily activities require it. How can one develop a lasting and reliable memory? It is possible to remember things from childhood that you are still able to relate to today.

However, it appeared that the majority of your past experiences had disappeared. Although our memories of what we were experiencing are not entirely gone (as some theories suggest), it is difficult to access them.

Theoretically speaking, there are two kinds of memory. The short term memory temporarily stores information. This may include the names you know from people at the bus stop, common things that happen every single day, and information you got from the book.

The long term memory stores information for a long duration. This type is the best for most situations.

But how do you develop a lasting and reliable memory?

Noa Rorrin (author) and Colin M. Macleod (author) conducted a study in order to answer the question.

Researchers found that the ability to speak loudly can help you retain the information.

This principle is not novel. According to psychologists and experts, this is known as the "production phenomenon". This suggests that our memory is stronger when we read loudly than when we read silently.

Colin M. Macleod is the co-author.

"Active involvement has been shown to improve memory and learning," says the study. The word is more distinct in longterm memory when it has an active measure or production element. This makes it memorable.

This is a valuable insight for students and everyone else. If you find yourself reading something or want to recall it, you can try saying it loud.

Unfortunately, it's not possible to do so in a library. Find somewhere that won't cause disturbances to others.

Strengthening Neural Connections

Running is beneficial for our health. Running helps our bodies stay active and healthy. Running has a positive impact not only on the outer part of the body, but also on your nervous system.

According to recent research, running can improve brain neural connections. Regular runners have a better brain connection than those who do nothing. In the brain region responsible for planning, decision making and emotional control, neural connections were stronger.

Dr. David Raichlen (lead author) said:

"One thing that drove this collaborative is that there have been recent proliferations of studies over 15 years that have shown that exercise and activity can have positive effects on the mind. However, most research has been done in seniors.

This is a crucial question that has not been fully explored.

Not only do we care about what's in the brains young adults, but it's also important to understand how your lifestyle can affect what happens in later years.

Healthier cognitive functioning can be indicated by healthier neural connections. A better memory is one benefit of having a strong neural network. The brain can store a lot more information if there are better neural connections.

But how did it happen? Dr. Raichlen explained:

"These repetitive activities can actually be complex cognitive functions, like planning and decision making, that could have effects on our brains."

Only a few studies, however, have looked into the neural effects that running has on runners. Many questions are still unanswered. However, the previous study offers us an important lesson.

The Best Exercise to Increase Long-Term Memory

According to the theory, we have two types or memory: the quick-term and long-term. The first can hold information in a very short period of time. The information held by the latter is for a much longer time.

A theory suggests that any information that comes into our heads will temporarily be stored in our short term memory. Due to its limited space, older memories become less useful as more information is received.

It is not possible to erase all the information. Some important information remains. In this instance, the information is believed to be in long-term storage.

Information that is stored in the long term memory can be retained for many decades.

These pieces of information need to be important for you. It could be a significant moment in your life like an accident, a birth present, or the name and address of your first girlfriend, boyfriend, or partner.

However, it can be very difficult to transfer short-term memory to longer-term. Many people, especially students have difficulty remembering.

A new study revealed a surprising solution. A group of researchers discovered that long-term memory is up to 20% when you combine weight training with exercise.

Participants were shown random photos and instructed not to memorize any.

One group of participants was instructed to make 50 leg extensions in resistance machine.

The second group, however, was instructed to use the leg extension chair but not sit for as long. Instead, their legs were moved by the machine.

The researchers asked the participants to recall what they had seen two days later.

The findings show that the majority of people who didn't complete the exercise only identified half the photos they saw. Only 60% of those who did it correctly were able to identify the photos. Exercise is better for memory.

How can exercise help improve memory? Any information, especially emotional materials, is more likely to stick in a heightened state of mind (exercise or stressful).

Audrey Duarte was one of the researchers who concluded:

"Even if we don't do expensive fMRI scans, these results help us understand which brain regions might be supporting the exercise-induced benefits.

These results are encouraging because they agree with rodent literature. This research pinpoints precisely which brain regions are involved in stress-induced benefits to memory due to exercise.

For those with memory damage or other mental impairments, the study may prove to be very helpful.

The best thing is that the research shows that you don't need to spend money on memory-enhancing medication. Simple knee bends can improve long-term memory.

Chapter 9: Memory Concept

Memory is a group of processes that helps you remember, recall, and identify past events. It is closely associated with attention and interest.

It is vital to life, as without it, there would be no way to think about the future or reflect on the past. Memory relies on the senses for data and facts that can be processed by the brain to create explanations.

The following factors influence the memory's efficiency:

Physical factors

Psychic Factors: Be realistic in your goals and aspirations, use critical thinking and problem solving.

Intellectual factors. True motivation, an enthusiasm to learn ....and a solid understanding Memorization is one of many fundamental factors.

Relationship between learning and memory

How do we learn

Learning is a process in which an organism learns from past life experiences. Learning something is about learning a new behavior. This means your brain will attempt to relate to past experiences if it has received a new experience via the sensory system.

To begin the learning journey, your brain uses memory. It uses this memory to recall the similar experiences it has previously had. This activates all the physiological as well chemical mechanisms to "mentally imagine" that memory.

The emotion of learning and the ability to remember

Emotion is energy to learn. Emotion allows us to remember and learn. If you have the right tools, such as emotion and attention, the circuit can be "activated". It prepares the body by creating molecules that enable synaptic communication. This will connect the new knowledge with previous neuronal schemes.

Memorization and emotion go together. This simply means that emotion lies at the core (or memorization) of this new concept. It is an ingredient that can be beneficial to both the teacher, and the learner. The foundation of emotion is the only thing that can sustain a true teaching process.

Neuroscience has taught us that binomial emotion/cognition is an indissoluble part of the brain's anatomical and functional design. This design, that has been passed down through millions of generations, shows that all sensory data passes through the limbic and acquires an emotional colour before it is processed in the cerebral cortex. These are the areas where ideas, abstracts, and the fundamental elements of thought can be created.

It is possible to have a range of phenomena when positive or negative emotions (affective valence) interact with memory processes such content, coding, recovery and other memory processes.

Coding that corresponds with the state and mind

We process information based upon the type of affective value that is consistent with our current state of mind during the memorization period. This causes the person to behave in accordance with what he expects.

Memory congruent to the state

During retrieval information, the emotional condition at the moment information is remembered can interact and affect the emotional content of that memory. In other words: When we are happy, the world is more pleasant and we recall more positive events from our past.

Memory is affected by how we think.

It is important to consider moods and how they affect the recovery and coding phases. These will help improve your ability of recall regardless of the affective tone. Since the emotional tone associated with an event will often be related to the person's emotional state during code, it is unlikely there will ever be a pure dependent-memory phenomenon.

Chapter 10: Studying Like a Superstar

This section will be the most important for you as you move forward in your studies. It will teach the best study habits and attitudes to help you get through your assignments, classes, and exams. To begin, you will need to establish new habits of study that are not familiar to you.

You'll find yourself overwhelmed with all the information and homework for your classes. If you don't manage it effectively, you will quickly fall behind. Once that happens, it can be very difficult to recover. Here are some tips that will help you prevent this from ever happening.

Complete your homework as soon as possible! Do your homework immediately if you're given a homework task for the week. Use your break to complete the task. You can finish your homework once you're home from school. I understand that it can be hard to come home from school and finish more studying, but it is much more rewarding to get your homework done quickly.

Establish a rigid schedule. You need to know the time and hours of your classes, as well as any part-time or other commitments. Once you have all that information, create a weekly timetable. You should now be in a position to identify any gaps in the week that you will have time for either study or leisure.

Both are important. However, you must assign the correct weight for each. Every day should be filled both with study and with play. You will feel overwhelmed if your entire day is filled with studying. However, if your whole day is filled with relaxation you will feel lazy and dread the next day.

Keep a calendar or checklist. There is no better feeling than writing out "30% Assignment Due" with a pen. A journal with all deadlines and tasks is a great way to organize your work. It will also give you a feeling of accomplishment when you have completed them. It's a way to get small wins on your road to great marks in your subjects. You can also create your own tasks and deadlines.

Studying in groups is the best way to learn. While you will most likely do your revision, study and cramming in your bedroom, you should make an effort to set up (and keep organized) a study team from each of the classes. Once you realize the struggles of understanding the subject, it won't be so lonely after all.

As you learn that different topics are easier to master than others, you will also find that there is a lot of synergy between you as you help each other with the parts you are having trouble understanding. You can also set shared goals for topics or tasks, and apply friendly pressure to each other to accomplish these goals. Studying will be more enjoyable when you are with other people, which can lead to greater retention of information.

Smart and hard work is key! Work smart and efficiently. It's important to make sure that you're only doing what you were designed when you study in your designated area. Do not let it become a gray space where you're either studying or procrastinating.

Use your study hot-streaks to your advantage! Do not stop if you find yourself in an unusual mood, where you can easily study anything and aren't tired or bored. Sometimes you may find yourself in a trance and can't stop studying. Studying high will help you understand complex topics better and make it easy to complete your homework. You shouldn't let this streak end just because your favorite program is on TV.

It is true that intelligence may vary. But high school students who succeed, regardless of their intelligence, are those who have a good studying plan in place and don't fall into the traps of procrastination. This trap is nothing else than laziness. It can be broken if we eliminate FOMO (fear that we will miss out) and our distractions.

This FOMO is the thoughts that are lingering in your mind when you study. It is the belief that everyone else is having fun while it is hard for you to concentrate. It gets worse on weekends or sunny day, and even more so on Friday and weekend nights. FOMO can be defeated by setting your study hours for the times you think your friends won't enjoy studying. If you have the time and energy to study late at night, go for it. Study when it is possible to wake up before the dawn.

It is second to be destroyed that distracting things. Put your phone away while you're studying to avoid distractions. If you have an urgent matter to discuss with someone, they'll call. Keep your phone off the line and don't scroll through Instagram, Facebook, or messages. Use your emails only for the purpose of what you are doing, and avoid browsing other sites that might be relevant to what it is you're doing. With a little self-restraint you can achieve a lot in a short period of time.

To keep distractions out of your study space, I suggest wearing headphones with some study-inducing music. If you can close your eyes and block out the outside, you'll be able enter a Zen state that allows you to take control of your learning domain.

It is important to get enough rest. It's possible to have to work until the wee hours to complete an assignment. Don't do this. Students are prone to abandoning assignments at the last moment and having to rely heavily on rushed works. It will happen again to you. Keep learning from it and doing work as soon as possible. It is important to get at least six to eight hours sleep every night. This is crucial for remembering, consolidating your knowledge, and maintaining a healthy, responsive head.

Chapter 11: Organizing Time

"He who rises later must trot the whole day. " - Benjamin Franklin

You will never find enough time for everything. Charles Buxton

Before we move on to organizing our time, I wanted to comment briefly on the Benjamin Franklin quote. It is so truthful and wise. Imagine that you have been overslept and that school starts in just 15 minutes. You rush to get out of bed and quickly change into your clothes. Because you don't have enough time to make a meal, you just grab the cash. You grab your backpack, and you sprint to the bus. Your mom will drive you if you miss the bus. You arrive at school late. You realize that homework was not done at home during the first period. You now get only partial credit and will have additional work. You are required to wait in line at lunch so that food can be prepared. This is a change from the normal practice of sitting down and sharing lunch with your friends. You probably get the point. Poor time management leads to you working harder and "trot", as Franklin puts it. This principle applies to more things than sleeping late. If you don't plan ahead to take on projects or tests, you might find yourself constantly stressed and scrambling.

The second quotation is equally wise. The second is equally important. It requires you to become more focused on your essential tasks and to schedule time for them. You can improve your life and productivity by focusing on your important tasks and setting goals.

This book is about developing habits. You only become as good as the habits you practice consistently. You can save time by creating study plans. Study plans allow you to incorporate the habit being proactive instead than reactive. Here are some quick tips to help you differentiate between proactive and reactive.

Pro vs. Re

Cross country is something I coach. Each of our 65 athletes is given a team uniform at the beginning and end of each season. I would ask runners for their size before handing out uniforms one by ones. Before we had 65 runners, this was all that was required. This was a terrible plan that didn't work when I had 40 runners the first year. It was reactive. It was a complete disaster when I handed out uniforms that night. The entire process took over an hour. I accidentally gave out the wrong size uniforms and was forced to respond to numerous emails from frustrated moms later that evening. I handed over the uniforms to the assistant coaches the next year. She was proactive. She created a spreadsheet listing each runner's size and order information. She then put everyone's uniform in bags and wrote the name of each runner on the outside. It took her only about an hour. On the night she handed out every runner's bag. It took only 10 minutes, and she received very few emails after that evening. The uniforms made it easy for moms to run and was a big hit with runners.

This is just one example illustrating the difference between being proactive or reactive. A study plan is a tool that can help you manage your study time more effectively. It will allow you to take control of your homework and give you enough time to study for tests and complete projects. It will help to organize your time and allow you to complete all of your work. Let's assume, for example that you glance at your study plan and see that there is a vocabulary exam in two days. If you like going for walks, you might grab your vocabulary flashcards to look at while you go. You'll be able to save time later on for the science project, while enjoying a nice walk.

Learning to be proactive & creating a study strategy

The best habit to develop is the ability to take the time and map out a study plan. A weekly study plan is a great way to reduce procrastination. Although it seems unnecessary, it only takes 15 minutes. If you have set study times, it will be easier to make sure you complete your work.

This is the first step to getting an overview of what's in store for you this week.

* Look for the tests you have included in your syllabus and/or on your agenda. Major tests are usually announced in advance by most teachers. You should give

priority to tests, as they make up a substantial portion of your grade.

* After testing, make sure to look out for any long-term projects.

* Make sure to review your agenda for any assignments.

* Check your to-do list.

Next, you will need to make a list with all your assignments, projects, or tests for the week. This will help to ensure that you don't forget any assignments. You can also fit them all into your study/homework.

Next, determine the time it will take to complete each task and plan your week accordingly. Let's examine a typical week and see how it can be organized in your planner. Looking at the agenda, it is clear that I have a science test and a math exam on Thursday. The homework for Friday will be math homework on Wednesday.

I think the science test involves the human body systems, as well notes on several pages. I think I can master the material in under two hours. It is in algebra so it will be challenging. It will likely require three hours of work. The paper in social studies should only take an hour.

Next, I prepare a rough week-end schedule, and then create a final schedule.

Monday

Tuesday

Wednesday

Thursday

Friday

Social studies paper 1 hour

Rough Draft

Social Studies Paper

Final Draft

Turn in Social studies paper

Science 30 Minutes

Science 30 Minutes

Science

1 hour

Test

No Homework

Math 30 Minutes

Math 30 Minutes

Math 1 hour

Math 1 hour

Test

Monday I can finish the rough draft and write my social studies paper in 50 to an-hour. I can also organize the science notes and study guide to see if they can be made into flashcards. Total time 30 minutes

I will finally start working on the study guides for math for 30 minutes. I make notes in my agenda and write down questions for my teachers or friends tomorrow.

This rough schedule shows that although it's a challenging week for testing, I don't stay up at night. I do each subject every day. My work is not always easy, and I sometimes need to work for a longer time one night. I am able to find some time riding to school, or in my homeroom. Preparing ahead will allow me to bring the materials along with me so that I can study when I have free time. This skill is necessary if you plan on taking honors or AP class. Even if your high school has advanced or honors classes, you still have the ability to participate in music, theater, or band. But, you'll need to be efficient.

My daughter took 9 AP courses and many honors classes in highschool. In addition, she ran cross-country and track for her highschool and swam. It taught her to be organized and to balance her studies with the activities and friendships.

When creating a study schedule, here are some things to be aware of:

Some teachers announce tests and classwork in the last seconds of their classes. A teacher who is like this can make it difficult to schedule extra time for the class. You may also need to visit their blog at least once a day to view any new updates. It's worth bookmarking this teacher's blog.

It is impossible to plan perfectly so it is important to be flexible.

A timer is a tool that many students find very helpful. They set the timer between 15 and 25 minute intervals, assign a goal, then take a quick rest when it goes off.

Include your weekly task list in your weekly study plan.

Your brain is not like a muscle. It can fatigue just as your muscles. From personal experience, I have found that it takes more effort for a marathon to run quickly than for the first couple miles. A similar principle applies to learning new material. The longer you study, the more effort it will take. Your most difficult work should be scheduled first. Then, the more demanding tasks can be assigned later. Most people will reverse this order and do their easiest tasks first. But by the time they get into the more challenging tasks, they are already mentally exhausted.

Learn how to manage time. Planning and scheduling your time is key to finding time you can use for study.

Here are some examples to help you maximize your time.

* Record notes and flashcards in your iPhone. You can listen to them while you work out.

* Bring a book or homework to do while you wait for the appointment.

* Read an assigned book, or study flashcards as you ride to after school activities. I'm confident you could ask America's top ten students about their studies. Most of these top students also ride to school.

* Don't waste time in school after taking a quiz or taking a test in another course. I have noticed that students in my class work at different speeds. Top students often ask me if it is possible to complete assignments from another class.

* Work during homeroom. Sometimes you can have a conversation with friends. But on days where there is a lot of homework

to do, take ten to 15 minutes to look at flashcards, study or jump start homework.

* The key to managing time effectively is having study material available and being able to find time throughout your day. Once you start looking for it, I believe you'll be surprised how much free time you have. Your brain can filter out unnecessary items and concentrate on the most important. For example, your dad might mention that he wants to purchase a new Jeep for the family. It's obvious that Jeeps are everywhere when you ride around town. Asking your brain to "start looking for free times in your schedule" will get your brain focused on this task, and you'll find that it starts finding them.

The Homework Filer: How to organize your homework

Many of my students have used this simple tool for homework over the past

20-years. This "homework folder" is a basic folder that has pockets on each side. You can also use bright colors, such as pink and red. This method has been used successfully by my daughter for many years.

You should write "Homework!" on the outside. On the inside, label each pocket with the words "To Be Done", as well as the right side with the word "Complete." Bring your agenda to class every day and make sure you have a list of homework due. If your teacher doesn't have the homework written on the whiteboard, then you can note that they are posting it to their blog.

The teacher will give you homework as a handout. Place it in your homework file on the right-hand side, marked "To Be Done". If you forget your planner or don't have one with you to class, you can simply write the homework on a sheet on notebook paper and place the "To Be Done" side. You can start your homework by getting out your homework file, emptying the "To Be Done" page. You will also need to grab your agenda to review any additional work.

After you have completed your homework, place it in the "Completed" area of your homework folder. When you are finished, take the homework folder out of your bag.

Your homework folder can be pulled out of your backpack and you can turn in your work at school the next morning.

Summary Notes

* Set up a weekly study program.

* Be proactive, not reactive, to maximize your time.

* Keep your homework organized by creating a homework notebook.

Chapter 12: Psychology Hacks

This chapter is probably the most critical in the book. You need to be able manipulate your own brain in order to truly become a great researcher. It is important to understand the inner workings of your brain. There are many psychological study strategies that you could use. These are just a handful of the psychological study techniques I have found the most useful over time.

Hack #3

Use mnemonics to remember things (and make sure they are dirty)

There are tons of books about memory and mnemonics that you can find. We aren't going to regurgitate all of the information. Instead, you'll find a few techniques that actually worked for us.

IN A NUTSELL Make them really naughty. This is one of the best ways they can be made outlandish.

Why? Over the course an academic year, you will have tons of facts. This sheer volume can cause confusion and be a real problem. It can also prevent you from recalling what you might need for a test.

Long-term, however, it can mean that you lose the knowledge you've acquired. I know exactly how you feel: you study all night for a test. Then, as soon as the exam is over, your brain quickly forgets everything.

Mnemonics devices are a wonderful biohack that prevents you from forgetting the things you have learned. The power of these guys is not to be underestimated. I still remember stuff that I studied nearly ten years ago as I prepared for the GRE. It was all thanks to mnemonics.

How? At its core, a mnemonic system is simply an association. This means you take what you want to recall and attach it to something else in the brain. As an example, I might picture a large man in a vest getting down funny to remember the definition of "divest".

It's a common misconception that when you hear the term "divest", your immediate thought is of a huge beefy man wearing a vest who is stripping in a comical way. This makes it easier to remember what "to remove from".

Did you notice how ridiculous this image was? That's the hack. Mnemonic devices perform better if your images are absurd. Make them really stupid.

This book is for the whole family.

If you aren't confident doing that (which it is), then this is totally cool! You can try to do something really, really crazy. Here are a few ideas for how to do it, and how I would use these to remind myself of the meaning of "divest".

Make an image of yourself in a wild setting. Imagine a pilot in a vest landing a plane at a strip made entirely from jello, because it's located on a planet that is made of the stuff.

Have fun with numbers! Wear a vest and sit down at a large plate of food with 1,000 bacon slices.

Make it ridiculous (having a vested in a piece of bacon that is 5 miles long)

These devices can be extremely powerful. Don't forget, this is just a small example of how mnemonics work. Learn more.

Hack #4

Study hard but not too long with study "bursts"

Many students that I have spoken to believe that studying hard is putting in lots of hours. You may find that studying for too long can actually make you less productive than studying in shorter bursts.

IN A NUTSHELL

Why? Have you ever driven when tired? If so, I hope that you stopped immediately. Driving while fatigued is just as dangerous as driving drunk, according to research. Your attention span decreases dramatically, and you lose nearly all your ability for focus.

It's not possible to study if you're tired. However, it can be dangerous. If you are bored and tired, it is likely that you won't be as effective at studying.

Remember to focus on small, powerful bursts when you study. It doesn't matter what you do, you can still make your study sessions short. If your study sessions are well-organized and efficient, even 5 minute sessions can be extremely productive.

This will make it much easier to study. You can easily study for 20-30 minutes (within reason, of course, if your schedule is crazy) and spend the rest of your time watching Netflix and munching cookies.

Warning: This won't work if there isn't enough study done in the short time.

How? Being organized is key to making the most of your short study breaks.

Make sure everything is set up and organized according what is important for you to study before you start. Place the important stuff first, and make sure all materials are available.

Start your serious study burst by knowing exactly what to do. You won't want to waste any time reading over notes. This isn't learning.

Do one activity per thing. If the most important thing to you is the names the first 10 American presidents are, then you could spend your entire 10 minutes studying detailed mnemonic devices and mnemonics of each president.

The second burst might be a 10 minute long time spent reciting those mnemonics aloud. In the final burst, you might spend the entire time reciting those things.

Does this make sense? These activities could be used for any type of strong learning strategy. The idea is to just act during those short bursts.

Pro tip! If you are suffering from anxiety or stress, you can spread your study sessions over a longer duration, giving yourself more time between. Enjoy relaxing, distracting and fun activities during the rest period. Balance will be a benefit when you return from studying.

Hack #5

Don't procrastinate by not planning (kinda).

Procrastinators love planning. If you are a procrastinator, I know exactly what it is like: you spend the whole day planning how you will accomplish your goals and then nothing happens.

Believe me, it isn't uncommon! There are many people who procrastinate. Over several years and particularly during my first semester in college, I had to discover the hard lesson that procrastination was not a good way to earn good grades. This is what I found.

IN A NUTSHELL The more you procrastinate the more you should plan.

You should only plan once you have started.

Why? The reason is simple: Procrastinators enjoy planning because it feels like they are making progress and don't have any work.

This isn't new. Let me tell you a story. Some people will go on a diet and plan out their exercise schedule, then tell everyone how excited they are to try this life-changing diet.

There is a reason. Studies show that when you tell others what you plan to do, they will compliment you on your motivation and tell tell you that you are doing a great work. It's a psychological advantage to have done it and not actually doing it.

Being psychologically content with yourself makes it difficult to stay motivated. When everyone is telling you

you're doing a great job, why would anyone tell you to go for it?!

Studying is the same as procrastination, even though it's more private. If you plan your studying to death, it is basically a way of congratulating your brain on all its work without really doing anything.

How? What are you supposed to do instead of plan? The short answer is that you should not plan. Here's how I mean it.

Stop planning if you are a procrastinator. Instead, start doing. Realize that you need to actually study, not plan.

It is important to start at all costs. It can be easier to relax and take less pressure. Take five minutes to open your book and watch a movie for five minutes before taking the test. Repeat the exercise at the end. This should give you an idea. Start is the most important aspect of life. If you don't plan, it can be very difficult to begin.

Planning can be very beneficial. It's important that you plan. Procrastinators must plan once they have begun to study. It should be kept very, very brief. I mean really concise. Don't forget to make a 5-point list of everything you want done during the study session. Planning for procrastinators will lead to a fatal trap. It shouldn't take you more than 30 minutes.

Hack #6

Gamify your education to maximize your productivity

Gamification may be a relatively new phenomenon. However, you can easily see it everywhere. There are many strategies that you may have seen before, if you've played any social game (e.g. "Share with three of your friends to unlock the super pig game token !").

But it's more than just for fun. It is becoming more popular than ever, and for good cause. Researchers have demonstrated that it is an extremely powerful motivator for any system.

IN A NUTSHELL

Why? Gamification is great because of a number of reasons. Gamification just makes things more fun. You can also see that this book makes studying less painful. Even though studying isn't fun by itself, if we make it at most a little funny, we can often get more out of it.

Gamification is an excellent way to achieve this. Even gamifying your studies on a very small scale can have an impact on how you feel about the task. Gamification helped me enjoy certain aspects of my education, which resulted in much higher grades.

Gamification also gives you a sense that you are accomplishing something. I can't emphasize how important this is-- especially when you are studying. It's not only boring, but it can also make studying feel pointless.

Sometimes it is difficult to stay motivated when things feel futile. Gamification gives you a sense of accomplishment which can help you psychologically power through material, especially if you are studying for longer periods.

How? The heart of most gamification systems is simply a series if rewards. This is how you get this. It's very simple.

This is fantastic news! It makes it super easy for most people to implement this on a small scale. You should reward yourself with great rewards. Great rewards are a great motivator.

Here's a quick example. One of my classmates was a biochemistry major. Her textbooks were very dense and large. So one of her main homework assignments every night was to just read hard-to-understand material.

Her solution? Gamify it! She placed one gummy bear at the top of each paragraph. Then, she would read each paragraph aloud. After she finished, she was allowed to eat a gummy bear. It was so easy and it was so much fun!

Pro tip! Mixing rewards can increase the gamification power. Reward yourself with small rewards when you accomplish big tasks, or a substantial reward when you complete an entire assignment.

To reward yourself for reading paragraphs, go with a friend to the movies and take three chapters. It can be as long or short as it feels like a great reward.

Hack #7

Repeat the steps loudly to help you remember them better

All people know that there are three kinds of learnings: auditory, visual and kinesthetic. Re-teaching offers a benefit almost everyone gets that isn't discussed often.

This idea states that if someone teaches you something, it will make it easier for you to learn it. It's been one of my best study methods in my solid study toolbox.

IN A NUSTSHELL. Repeat what you have just said to someone else, to get a better understanding and to commit them to your memory.

Why? The brain is incredibly impacted by the knowledge you share with others. It is generally much more efficient than just trying to memorize things.

This is mainly because instead of simply memorizing a fact, it's important to communicate it to others. You will have to put the information in context, answer questions about it, and finally fill in gaps in your knowledge.

It gives your memory more items to hold on to as it attempts to recall information. So, for example, if your memory is struggling to remember what you said about the French Revolution when you were explaining it to your roommate while taking a test you will have many more points of reference.

I wish that I would have learned this sooner. I discovered how effective this was after becoming a teacher. The first semester I taught was my best yet.

How? There are a few ways you can do this but the most important is to shout it out.

You will find it easier to master your skills if someone is there to help, but this is not essential. A girlfriend or boyfriend? Get your girlfriend or boyfriend to come sit down with you as you talk about the French Revolution.

Have a roommate Get them dinner and force them into listening. You get it. You'll find people willing to help you.

But, you can do this all by yourself. Stand up and give the speech as if you were talking to a friend. It is a good idea to tell it like you are talking to a 6 year old. This will require you to reduce the content down to a manageable level.

Chapter 13: Types of Learning Styles

There were assumptions that everyone learned new materials the same way. Scott Black was the Human Behavior Specialist who put Howard Gardner's research into practical use.

He was first to identify a consistent and predictable way to measure a person's learning style.

The process starts by taking the fingerprints. Black prepares a 36-page report in 24-48 hours. It reveals which of the eight types of learners the individual is, as well as how he/she processes visual, kinesthetic and auditory information.

Different learning styles

There are different learning styles.

Verbal (Linguistic)

Visual (Spatial).

Aural (Auditory/Musical).

Logical (Mathematical).

Physical (Kinesthetic).

Social (Interpersonal).

Solitary (Intrapersonal).

Naturalistic

Let's learn about them one at a time.

1. Verbal (Linguistic)

Verbal learning styles teach you how to use linguistic skills such reading, writing speaking or listening. Linguistic learners are commonly associated with public speaking. Journalism, writing, debate, and writing.

Characteristics in Verbal Learners

They enjoy reading and writing.

They can write and speak for themselves.

They like rhymes.

They love to learn new words and know a lot about a lot of vocabulary.

If you are a Linguistic Student, then you are a Linguistic Teacher.

To comprehend something, you can read aloud. You might prefer someone to relay the information verbally.

2. Visual (Spatial).

A visual style of learning means that you can learn the most by looking at an image. This allows you better to understand the information. You might also write or draw your thoughts in order to organize them.

What Characteristics are Visual Learners?

They have a keen sense of direction

They enjoy drawing, coloring, and doing a lot of doodling.

They can easily see plans, objects, or outcomes.

Maps are more useful than the average when it comes down to their use.

Spatial learners are those who have mastered spatial learning.

You prefer to process the information using pictures, mindmaps, images and pictures.

3. Aural (Auditory/Musical)

You learn with sound, rhythm or melody in the aural style of learning. Are you aware that almost all musicians fall within this category? Music doesn't distract students, but rather helps them process the information more effectively.

Aural Learners: What Characteristics?

They love learning when the music plays in the background

Sometimes music can elevate their emotions

They have a good sense for pitch or rhythm.

It is possible that the songs and jingles which they hear often circulate in them without prompting.

You can be an Aural Learner if

If you like rhythms or are good at remembering things, then rhythms may be your preferred method of learning.

4. Logical (Mathematical).

This learning style involves learning by categorizing and classifying things. Logical learners are better than anyone at understanding patterns and equations, numbers, or relationships. Most logical learners work as engineers, scientists, mathematicians, or other technical professionals.

Logical Learners - Characteristics

They prefer to classify and group the information in order better understand it

They are comfortable with complex calculations

They are excellent at organizing and ranking itineraries and agendas.

When they discover the solution to a problem, they enjoy developing solutions.

Logical Learner

It is essential to understand the systems, reasoning, and the larger picture behind any information/ concept before you can learn.

5. Physical (Kinesthetic).

Learning in the kinesthetic way is when you actually do it. These learners are more scientific than the rest and like to interact with real objects to learn. The majority of physical learners are interested, among other things, in manufacturing and arts.

Characteristics among Kinesthetic Learners

They love sports and outdoor activities.

They see, and they also understand the material world around.

They are good at understanding the body language and using it effectively

They enjoy solving jigsaws or building models.

If you can use your kinesthetic senses to learn, then you are a Kinesthetic Lesser.

Learn something only by doing it alone. You must also be able to use your hands to communicate and remain in motion.

6. Social (interpersonal).

The interpersonal approach to learning is one that encourages interaction with others. You love to share stories and work in groups. The learners in this group are a natural group worker, a team player, or a good leader.

Characteristics and characteristics of interpersonal learners

They love socializing after work

They are good listeners

They like to play in teams, or group sports.

Others look forward to them for advice.

If you're an Interpersonal Learner

You are comfortable working in groups.

7. Solitary (Intrapersonal).

This type of learning requires you to be independent. Or you might learn best when you are on your own. This kind of learner is usually an introvert, although it doesn't always happen. Some people are extroverts when in social situations but prefer to be alone while they learn.

Characteristics Of Intrapersonal Learners

They prefer to avoid the crowds even when traveling.

They spend their time self-analyzing.

They strive to improve and document, write or record their personal thoughts.

They love to think on their own.

You are an Intrapersonal Student if

You can study alone or in a group to understand information.

8. Naturalistic

Naturalistic learning is about learning new things and information through direct contact with nature. It is also the learning style that scientists use to discover new things.

Characteristics Of Naturalistic Learners

They like to see the world around their home.

They love to experience new things

They believe that experimentation allows them to discover the best knowledge and information.

They enjoy being outdoors.

Naturalistic Learner

The ability to discern and observe the elements of nature is amazing.

QUIZ TIME

WHAT IS YOUR LEARNING TTYLE?

The quiz has eight (8) sections. There are three (3) statements per section. Each sentence needs to be read, ranked and ranked according to its importance.

1 = This is not me.

2 = This is a sentence that describes me somewhat.

3 = This sentence describes me perfectly.

Section I

It's great when you can mentor others. [1] [2] [3]

You like stories and metaphors. [1] [2] [3]

Communication is a skill that you are skilled at. [1] [2] [3]

Section II

You enjoy paintings, visual arts and jigsaw puzzles. [1] [2] [3]

Scribbles, diagrams, and other visual aids are helpful in communicating concepts and ideas. [1] [2] [3]

You love to, and often take photographs with a camera. [1] [2] [3]

Section III

Music is a way to help you remember your past. You develop strong emotions. [1] [2] [3]

You can sing well and are skilled with musical instruments. [1] [2] [3]

Music is something that you love to listen to, regardless of whether you are studying, working, or traveling. [1] [2] [3]

Section IV

You enjoy playing logic and strategy games like Chess. [1] [2] [3]

Step-by-step methods are preferred for solving problems. [1] [2] [3]

You enjoy pointing out logic flaws within the activities of others. [1] [2] [3]

Section V

Art, sculpture and metalworking are your favorite hobbies. [1] [2] [3]

To truly understand something, you like to touch it. [1] [2] [3]

When communicating, you may use hand gestures or keep your body language physical. [1] [2] [3]

Section VI

You enjoy social events and parties. [1] [2] [3]

Many close friends surround you. [1] [2] [3]

You enjoy playing team sports like soccer and basketball. [1] [2] [3]

Section VII

You may keep a personal journal in which to record your thoughts. [1] [2] [3]

You like to read self-help literature. [1] [2] [3]

You like to do things on your own without having to involve others. [1] [2] [3]

Section VIII

It is easy to feel at peace when you are in contact with nature. [1] [2] [3]

Instead of looking at other people's experiences as a guide, you want to be able to see things for yourself. [1] [2] [3]

Outdoors, you feel confident. [1] [2] [3]

Solution

Each section represents the learning style described below:

Verbal (Linguistic)

Visual (Spatial).

Aural (Auditory/Musical).

Logical (Mathematical).

Physical (Kinesthetic).

Social (Interpersonal).

Solitary (Intrapersonal).

Naturalistic

Calculate the total score in each section.

SECTION TOTAL SCORE

Verbal (Linguistic)

Visual (Spatial).

Aural (Auditory/Musical).

Logical (Mathematical).

Physical (Kinesthetic).

Social (Interpersonal)

Solitary (Intrapersonal).

Naturalistic

Find the top 3 sections scoring high.

Chapter 14: Supplementation & Nootropics

While a healthy lifestyle is a great way to improve your long-term mental and physical health, it's important to do more.

How many times can you recall seeing a movie about a fictional drug or technology that improves the human potential? Humans have always loved the brain and the idea that it can be used to its full potential. "Smart drugs" (also known as nootropics) and supplements are created for this purpose. Although they do not specifically target the brain, some of these supplements affect vital body functions that directly affect the brain.

Cognitive enhancers shouldn't be confused by nootropics. Nootropics can be described as cognitive enhancers. But not all cognitive enhancers qualify as nootropics. A cognitive enhancer is an umbrella term that encompasses all substances that can improve or stimulate the brain functioning of a person.

Tip. To be sure you are taking the right diet, nootropics, or supplements, you will need to keep track in your personal brain health journal of all changes. It can either be written on a personal computer or a physical notebook. Your personal information's privacy and accessibility are entirely your choice.

Supplements

It is a good idea to consult your doctor before using supplements. Your doctor will advise you whether your body is well-prepared to take supplements. Your doctor should also have the ability to give proper dosage instructions.

Vitamin E- Vitamin E, also known as Vitamin E, is a powerful antioxidant found in food such as cereals. Vitamin E supplements, which are quite common, can help you ensure you are getting enough without any redundancies or conflicts in your diet. Vitamin E is used to treat diseases of the nervous system like dementia (Alzheimer's Disease, etc. Vitamin E is used to treat Parkinson's disease, epilepsy and Parkinson's. It can also help with complications in the heart or blood, and many other ailments. Vitamin E is vital to the health of body cells. Vitamin E should be consumed by adults, males and women.

Vitamin C- Humans can only get vitamin C through food sources or supplements. Vitamin C is critical for one's immune system. Vitamin C can protect against common ailments like stomach aches, skin infections, common colds, and common colds. It has also been proven to be beneficial in treating depression and other cognitive problems.

Creatine, a Creatine supplement was initially designed to increase physical strength in athletes. After further research, it has been proven to be beneficial for memory and attention span. It has been suggested that it can be used in Huntington's disease treatment, which can result in a permanent disability of a person's ability to walk and talk. Creatine supplements are available in many varieties, usually around 5,000mg per person.

Fish Oil: Fish oil, which is made from either fish meats and supplements, supports the health of brain cells. Improvement in blood circulation is one benefit of fish oil. Fish oil is effective in treating blood pressure, preventing strokes, improving digestion and reducing inflammations. Studies also reveal a direct connection between fish oils and brain volume. This is especially true in the cerebral cortex and hippocampus which are areas of the brain that are responsible memory and thinking.

Alpha-Lipoic Acid – Also referred to as ALA. This antioxidant has been proven effective in protecting the brain, nerve tissues, and other organs from injury. It is used for the treatment of certain nerve disorders in Europe. There is evidence that Alpha-Lipoic Acid supplements may reduce the risk of developing dementia over the long-term. There is currently no recommendation for ALA Supplements. Ask your doctor.

Calcium - Calcium promotes strong bone and tooth structure, and helps keep your heart, blood, nerves, and brain healthy. Calcium can be easily obtained from milk or other daily products.

Nootropics

A nootropic is a kind of drug (artificial/natural chemicals) commonly known as smart drugs, memory enhancers/intelligence enhancers, and neuro-enhancers. Nootropics act in a variety of ways, including stimulating nerve growth, improving oxygen circulation in brains, or altering neurotransmitters, enzymes and hormones in brains.

There are currently many nootropic drug options that can improve concentration, alertness. memory and confidence. Nootropics are well-known for their ability to treat cognitive disorders such Alzheimer's or Parkinson's.

Researchers and users are discovering more practical uses for the nootropics. Nootropics are gaining popularity among both students and professionals for their ability to boost productivity. These claims have scientific support, as well the testimonials of thousands of people who have used them.

Modafinil

This nootropic can often be compared to the NZT48 (Limitless 2012). The NZT-48 enhances the mental functioning of people and "unlocks 100% brain capacity."

Modafinil doesn't have the exact same effects in reality as the movie drug. Modafinil acts as a wakefulness-promoting stimulant. It can be used medically for bipolar depression, depression, opiate or cocaine dependence and Parkinson's Disease, Schizophrenia. It is also used as an alternative for amphetamine by the military to keep troops awake without compromising mental clarity and focus.

Modafinil users have numerous benefits for their every-day use, including:

Increased Visual Focus- After 3 minutes, users will notice a sharpening in their vision and a greater level of focus. Modafinil wakefulness can increase awareness of one's surroundings, which can be both a positive and negative thing. The user may find it easier to focus while engaging in visual activity. However, flashing bright lights, noticeable visual disturbances, and flashing lights can easily distract him.

However Comprehension improvement - There are many stimulants that improve mental clarity as well as nootropics that positively impact decision-making skills. This boost can be useful for studying or organizing your work load, as well as making business-related judgments.

Modafinil Increases Physical Capabilities – Modafinil offers a slight resistance for fatigue. This is an extremely useful feature for anyone who works out. Modafinil will not increase physical strength. However its wakefulness effects and stimulation effects can allow people to accomplish more than usual.

Modafinil Users Experience Improved Social Skills Modafinil patients experience an increase of confidence and motivation that allows them be more engaged in conversations and pay more attention to various topics.

Modafinil can improve mood. This effect is the least known of all Modafinil's positive effects. This is not because Modafinil does not have a mood-improving effect, but because most users (especially new users) are so distracted with higher performance that they fail to notice their moods. Cognitive enhancements such a better analysis, reasonability. comprehension, and focus will make it easier to be more motivated.

Appetite suppression - Appetite suppression may be a side effect in many stimulants. It is often considered a positive by many users. Modafinil can suppress the appetite, so users don't feel deprived of food.

Modafinil Side Effects

Modafinil occasionally causes mild side effect on some users. There have also been rare cases of moderately disruptive side affects. The most common side effects from taking Modafinil are headaches (34% for 934 subjects) and nausea (11% for 934 subjects). These side effects are often mild and easily tolerated, although further risks are being researched.

Euphoria can also happen when Modafinil dosages are excessively high. Modafinil 600 mg (200mg is the standard dosage) produces mild euphoria. Modafinil 1,200mg or more can cause extreme euphoria. Modafinil should not be given to children under the age of 18. Modafinil can be used for up to 12 hours. This makes it unwise to use the drug in the afternoon.

Modafinil users experience the wakefulness effect, but other effects can vary. Modafinil users generally experience positive effects. However, many users have reported feeling satisfied with their drug.

Adderall

Adderall, also known under the name of amphetamine mixture salts (AMS), is a stimulant most well-known because it has a strong effect on the central nervous. Adderall can also be used for the treatment of narcolepsy as well as attention deficit hyperactivity disorders (ADHD). Some patients may also take it to manage depression.

Adderall as well as Modafinil provide a boost to cognitive performance, working memory, and mood. Modafinil is a generic compound of amphetamine.

Adderall increases adrenaline's production. This alters heart rate and bloodflow, giving the user an extra energy boost. Many people experience an increase in attention and concentration. This effect is similar to Modafinil and is highly sought-after by both students as well as working people. Adderall is often prescribed to athletes for improved physical performance.

Adderall could be potentially dangerous if used long-term. Adderall is known for causing complications in the cardiovascular systems, sometimes leading to strokes and heart conditions.

Modafinil has been proven to be safer than other stimulants. Modafinil users are not likely to develop psychological or physical dependence from Adderall.

Adderall Side Effects

Adderall can cause side effects such as the following. You should stop using it immediately and consult your doctor.

Fast/Uneven Heartbeat

Fainting

Tremors

Seizure

Mild to Moderate Side Effects

Headache

Impotence

Hallucinations

High blood pressure

Blurred vision

Chest Pain

Piracetam

Piracetam works by increasing brain metabolism. This cognitive enhancer is widely used to improve memory. It improves oxygen flow and blood circulation in the brain as well as the glucose processing.

Piracetam, which works on the cerebral cortex, is medically prescribed to treat cortical marrow clonus. The most common symptom in cortical myoclonus are the involuntary movements of the arms, legs and hands.

The drug can also be used to treat other cognitive impairments like:

Alzheimer's disease

Raynaud disease

Senile Dementia

OCD, Obsessive Compulsive Disorder

Memory loss, short term

Dyslexia

Alcoholism

Circulatory Disorders

It is clinically cleared for use in Europe. Asia. And South America. This includes the above-mentioned conditions. It can also serve as a nootropic.

Piracetam Effects

Piracetam appears to enhance the interaction between left and right brain hemispheres (IntelligenceQuotient) by increasing cerebral blood phospholipid and cell membrane fluidity. This, in turn, has been supported by research.

Piracetam, a potent antioxidant, is extremely beneficial in achieving improved cognitive functioning. Piracetam can cause very few side reactions, with the most common being nervousness (and weight gain).

Piracetam comes in many brands today. There are different dosages for adults and children. You should check each brand's instructions.

You should limit your use of nootropics, as you would with other substances. Cognitive enhancers can have short-term results. Don't take too many of them. Instead, concentrate on how you will use them for as long as they last. For example, nootropics should be used only for productive tasks such as exercising, writing, and studying. This will reduce the possibility of suffering from unwanted side effects.

Conclusion

The goal of your study is to achieve it. You can be encouraged to study by others, but the ultimate decision is yours. You must remember that your study is solely for you. This is also true for anyone else. If you are studying for the sake of impressing others, you might have to use a lot less steam. This is a solo effort.

In order to ensure that you study as much as possible, I would like to share two points with you. For you to get the best results, it is important that you keep your focus on what you are doing. The other is to practice until you get it right.

Happy studying!

www.ingramcontent.com/pod-product-compliance
Lightning Source LLC
Chambersburg PA
CBHW050025130526
44590CB00042B/1905